Nature's Window
FROGS

Nature's Window

FROGS

Sheila Buff

**Andrews McMeel
Publishing**

Kansas City

INTRODUCTION

Frogs populated the earth years ago, alongside the dinosaurs. The dinosaurs are gone, but frogs live on today. These small amphibians are mostly denizens of watery places—rain forests, swamps, ponds—but they are found in virtually every part of the globe, including deserts and the Arctic.

Frogs are also global in folklore: They are featured in European fairy tales and are

Frogs of the tropical rain forest in South America often use water-filled bromeliads—plants that grow on other plants—to lay their eggs. Here a leaf frog clings to a bromeliad in Ecuador.

symbols of good luck in Japan; in ancient Egypt, they were fertility symbols; Native Americans believed frogs predicted rain by their croaking.

Frogs also have a negative image. A plague of frogs descended on the Egyptians in the Bible. European witches were said to use frogs to cast spells, while in China toads are seen as poisonous. To many, frogs are cold, slimy, and repellent. On the other hand, frogs' legs are considered a delicacy—to the point that over-collection for cooking is endangering some species.

One of the most fascinating aspects of frogs is their amazing variety. Some are so colorful they seem to be painted. Glass frogs are green on top, but translucent from below, clearly revealing their internal organs. And even the most ordinary frogs have intricate patterns of skin color, strikingly colorful eyes, and fascinating life cycles.

THE FROG FAMILY

Frogs are members of the large animal class called amphibians—creatures that begin life as legless tadpoles or larvae in the water and metamorphose (change their shape) as they grow to adulthood, becoming land-dwelling, four-legged animals with moist skins. Amphibians include newts and salamanders, but most are

Camouflage helps conceal frogs from predators such as snakes and birds—and lets them ambush their prey. This Solomon Islands leaf frog is the same color as the leaf litter it rests on.

members of the order Anura—frogs and toads. Around the world, there are some four thousand different Anura species; about eighty-five

of these are found in North America. New frog species are discovered fairly often—at a rate of about ten or more a year—especially in tropical regions.

In general, frogs have smooth, moist (or even slimy) skin and move by jumping on long hind legs. Toads generally have dry, warty skin and move with short hops or by walking on shorter hind legs. The line between frogs and toads isn't a sharp one, though, and many fall somewhere on a continuum, with characteristics of both. When scientists talk about

A red-eyed tree frog of Central America has superb night vision. On its nocturnal hunting expeditions it will open its pupils so wide that the red iris will almost disappear.

frogs, they usually mean both frogs and toads.

Frogs need plenty of moisture to survive and breed, so they are most often found near permanent sources of fresh water such as swamps, streams, ponds, and lakes (there are no saltwater frogs). Almost all frogs are excellent swimmers, but they don't stay in the water all the time. In fact, frogs can drown if they can't eventually climb up onto water plants or dry land.

Most frogs live in warm, moist regions, but many species are found in more extreme

Many frogs, such as this Cuban tree frog, are powerful jumpers. Unusually large for a member of the tree frog family, these frogs are often more than five inches long.

climates. A number of frogs live in very hot, dry places. They survive the arid desert heat with a variety of different strategies. Spadefoot toads of the Colorado Desert, for example, estivate (sleep during the summer— the opposite of hibernate) in underground burrows during the dry season. They can survive there, without food or water, for at least two years. When they hear rain, they leave their burrows and resume normal life.

Frogs survive freezing winters in cold regions by hibernating in burrows or in the

More than 120 members of the sedge frog family, including this painted reed frog, are found in the marshy regions of sub-Saharan Africa. Most are brightly colored with prominent spots or stripes.

The glass frog family, found in the moist regions of Central and South America, has about sixty-four species, including this frog, HYLA PUNCTATA. Almost all glass frogs are a vivid green and have nearly transparent skin.

mud at the bottom of ponds and lakes. Some species even make a sort of antifreeze in their blood.

Most frogs are on the small side. The common spring peeper, for example, is only about an inch long. The world's smallest frog is *Psyllophryne didactyla*, found in Brazil. Adults of this species are only about a third of an inch long. The adult *Sminthillus limbatus*, found in Cuba, measures just half an inch long.

In North America, the bullfrog is the largest frog, reaching a body length of about eight inches. The largest frog in the world is the rare African giant frog, also called the goliath frog; it reaches a body length of more than fourteen inches and a weight of eight pounds.

Frogs have very thin, moist skin unprotected by hair, feathers, or scales. Although they are cold-blooded, frogs don't bask in the sun to raise their body temperature like other cold-blooded animals because this dries their skin too much. Frogs have lungs for breathing, but they don't have any ribs. To get enough oxygen, they must also absorb some through their thin skin.

F ROG ANATOMY

Frogs have very sharp eyesight. Their bulging eyes, generally mounted on top of the head, can see in almost any direction, including to the rear. Each eye can focus independently on objects as distant as forty or fifty feet. Frogs seem to be somewhat farsighted—they see their prey best when it is several feet away, and may not see it at all if it is right under their noses.

Frogs catch food with long, sticky tongues. They dart their tongues out very rapidly—

The tomato frog is a large frog (about three to four inches long) found only on the island of Madagascar. Its name comes from its strong resemblance to a large, ripe tomato.

faster than the human eye can see—and flip the food into their mouths. Almost all frogs are carnivores, eating insects, worms, spiders, and other small prey. Larger frogs eat larger food. Bullfrogs, for example, eat insects, but they also devour mice, smaller frogs, and even birds. The only limit is the size of the victim. Frogs don't have real teeth, so they have to swallow their prey whole. If it's alive and can fit into a frog's mouth, it will be eaten. Because frogs absorb water through their skin, they don't need to drink.

Most frogs have legs that are well adapted for climbing or jumping. Climbing frogs, such as tree frogs, have adhesive pads on their toes that help them cling to trees. Jumping frogs have powerful hind legs that propel them forward very quickly. The world record for a frog triple jump is more than thirty feet, set by a South African sharp-nosed frog. When measured as a multiple of body length, however, the world champion jumper is the eastern cricket frog. This small frog, only about an inch long, can leap forty-eight times its length in a single jump.

CROAKS AND COLORS

The sounds of frogs croaking, chirping, calling, and otherwise making noise fill the night just as birdsong fills the day. And just as every bird species has a different song, every frog species has a different call. As a rule, the larger the frog, the louder and longer the call. The sounds vary considerably, from trills and chirps to whistles, barks, grunts, and peeps. In North America, the classic "ribbit" sound is made only by the Pacific tree frog.

In the early spring in North America, sometimes even before the ice has melted, the chorus of mating tree frogs fills the night. This gray tree frog has inflated its vocal sac to make its loud trilling call.

The primary purpose of frog calls is to attract a mate. During the breeding season, male frogs near water sing their mating call in loud—sometimes deafening—choruses. Females are attracted to the sound and arrive to mate.

Frogs produce their varied calls using their vocal cords, but they sing with their mouths closed. To amplify the volume and resonance of their calls, male frogs use their vocal sacs, loose folds of skin in their throats. Some frogs can inflate their vocal sacs like balloons; others just expand their throats to both sides.

Female frogs don't make mating calls the way males do, but both sexes produce a variety of other noises. Distress calls are used to frighten off attackers such as snakes. These calls can sound remarkably like human screams and are probably the origin of many scary tales about swamp monsters. Alarm calls are loud yelps made by startled frogs, usually just before they leap for safety into the water.

To hear all that croaking, frogs have ears on their

Worldwide, there are more than six hundred species of tree frogs, including this yellow one clinging to a tree trunk in the Amazon. Most tree frogs are quite small (no more than two or three inches long) and are found in tropical rain forests, but a number of species are found in temperate parts of the world.

heads behind their eyes. A round membrane similar to a human ear drum, a frog's ear is attuned to the calls of its species. It hears those sounds extremely well, but otherwise frogs don't have especially good hearing. When frogs jump away from a threat, it's usually because they have seen it, not heard it.

Overall, frogs are generally brownish, gray, or green, the better to blend in with their environments and avoid being eaten by predators such as herons, snakes, raccoons, and the like. For the same reason, frogs tend to have white or light-colored underparts, so that predators from below (large fish such as pike, for example) can't see them very well.

Some frogs, however, have bright colors that are used to avoid enemies. Poison dart frogs, for instance, are very vivid as a warning to would-be predators. Other frogs have brightly colored limbs or underparts that they "flash" at an enemy just before they jump away. The flash of color seems to confuse the predator and gives the frog a chance to escape.

FROG LIFE CYCLE

The breeding season for frogs in temperate regions lasts from early spring to late summer. In tropical and desert regions, the breeding season generally corresponds to the rainy season. When the breeding season arrives for a frog species, the males gather together and call loudly and continuously to attract the females. For several days (or even longer), the frogs are in a frenzy of activity, attempting to mate with anything that is approximately their own size.

The green frog is commonly found in ponds and lakes of the eastern United States. It lays its eggs in still, shallow water. When disturbed, the frogs let out a piercing cry and jump into the air.

Frogs must lay their eggs in water or a moist place. The male frog climbs onto the female's back and seizes her firmly from behind, an embrace known as amplexus. As the female releases her eggs, the male fertilizes them. The jellylike eggs are expelled in clusters or long strings, usually in very large numbers: A single female may produce several thousand. Most of the eggs don't hatch, but are eaten by predators such as fish and ducks.

The eggs grow rapidly and usually hatch within a week to produce larvae—better known as tadpoles.

Looking like fish, the tadpoles have long tails and gills for breathing and survive on algae and other vegetable matter.

Tadpoles evolve rapidly into frogs. Their tails shrink, they grow legs, and they start to spend some time out of the water. The metamorphosis usually takes a couple of weeks, but some species grow even more rapidly. Others, such as the bullfrog, take up to two years to metamorphose.

For the most part, parent frogs produce the eggs and then have nothing to do with their offspring. There

Tree frogs are found in an astonishing range of colors, as these orange-footed tree frogs show. The colors can vary considerably within each species—some individuals are more brightly colored than others —and by region. During the day, they perch on a leaf and fold their brightly colored legs in under their bodies. From above, the sleeping frogs are hard to distinguish from the leaf, protecting them from predators.

are many very interesting exceptions to this rule. The female marsupial frog of Suriname, for example, carries some sixty fertilized eggs on the spongy skin of her back for two to four months until they hatch and the larvae have grown into fully formed miniature frogs. The gastric brooding frog (now extinct) of Australia carried her thirty or so tadpoles in her stomach for about eight weeks until they emerged from her mouth as froglets. During this time, the mother frog turned off her stomach acid and ate nothing.

Most frogs don't pay any attention to their eggs after they are laid, but this marsupial frog carries her eggs on special tissue on her back until they hatch and grow from tadpoles into tiny froglets.

POISON DART FROGS

Some of the tiny, colored frogs of the rain forests of Central and South America merit special attention because of their poisonous skin secretions. These frogs are known as poison dart frogs, because native peoples use the poison to tip blowgun darts.

To date, there are about 135 different poison dart frog species (scientists are still discovering new ones). All secrete chemicals of various kinds, but only about 55 species are known to be dan-

Tiny but deadly, poison dart frogs are found in the rain forests of Central and South America. Their vivid colors, such as the blue-yellow of this frog, warn off potential predators.

gerously toxic. The frogs are small and are very brightly colored—a warning to potential predators. The poisons secreted are among the most toxic known. A tiny drop of poison from *Phyllobates bicolor*, found in western Colombia, is enough to kill a human. Dangerous as the toxins are, they may also have valuable medical uses as more than three hundred different compounds have been identified in the secretions, including some that have potential as painkillers, heart stimulants, and muscle relaxants.

Poison dart frogs are very small; most are no more than an inch or so long, like this Ecuadorean frog on a mushroom. It is thought that poisonous secretions protect the frog against harmful bacteria.

Frogs in Danger

Researchers increasingly report that frogs of all sorts are becoming harder to find. A number of frog species have become extinct just in the last few decades. The golden toad of Costa Rica was discovered in 1964 but had virtually disappeared by the late 1980s. Deformed frogs with missing or useless limbs have become increasingly common. Habitat destruction and alteration is a major cause because frogs spend their lives both in water and on land; they are doubly exposed to danger from pollutants.

Another important factor may be global warming, which disrupts the water supplies frogs depend on so heavily. The thinning of the ozone layer, acid rain, rain forest destruction, harmful bacteria, and introduced predators also play a significant part in frog loss.

Overall, the populations of frogs and other amphibians throughout the world are in dangerous decline as their habitats are lost or degraded. Their only hope is for people to recognize the damage the destruction of frog habitats is doing to frogs.

The green frog is one of the most abundant frogs in the northeastern United States, but its numbers may be declining sharply, like those of many other frog species. Overall, by some estimates, nearly a third of all frog species in the United States may be in danger.

Photography credits

All images provided by ENP Images except page 13.

© Pete Oxford: pages 2, 4, 12, 16–17, 20, 28–29, 36–37, 39, 43;

© Gerry Ellis: page 9; © Steve Gettle: pages 10, 24, 32, 46–47;

© Joe McDonald: page 13; © Michael Durham: page 40;

Front jacket: © Steve Gettle;

Back jacket: © Pete Oxford.

www.andrewsmcmeel.com

ISBN: 0-8362-5300-0

Printed in Singapore

First U.S. edition

1   3   5   7   9   10   8   6   4   2

Editor: Deri Reed
Art Director: Tomek Lamprecht
Designer: Paola Pelosi

Produced by Smallwood & Stewart, Inc., New York City